CAUSES AND REMEDI

OF THE

PRESENT CONVULSIONS:

A DISCOURSE

BY REV. JOHN C. LORD, D. D.

BUFFALO;
JOSEPH WARREN & CO., BOOK AND JOB PRINTERS, 178 WASHINGTON STREET,

1861.

CAUSES AND REMEDIES

OF THE

PRESENT CONVULSIONS:

A DISCOURSE

BY REV. JOHN C. LORD, D. D.

BUFFALO:
JOSEPH WARREN & CO., BOOK AND JOB PRINTERS, 178 WASHINGTON STREET,

1861

A DISCOURSE

DELIVERED ON THE DAY OF FASTING, HUMILIATION AND PRAYER APPOINTED BY THE PRESIDENT OF THE UNITED STATES, AND BY THE MODERATOR OF THE GENERAL ASSEMBLY OF THE PRESBYTERIAN CHURCH IN THE UNITED STATES OF AMERICA, JANUARY 4TH, 1861;

BY JOHN C. LORD, D. D.,

PASTOR OF THE CENTRAL PRESBYTERIAN CHURCH, BUFFALO, N. Y.

"When thou passest through the waters, I will be with thee, and through the rivers they shall not overflow thee. When thou walkest through the fire thou shalt not be burned: neither shall the flame kindle upon thee. Fear not, for I am with thee. I will bring thy seed from the East, and gather thee from the West. I will say to the North, give up, and to the South, keep not back."—[*Isaiah*, XLIII, 2, 5, 6.

It would seem from the amazement and alarm, which have resulted from the present convulsed state of the nation, that the people of this country have anticipated an exemption from those calamities, which, in the course of the divine providence, have accompanied, and for a time checked, the outgrowth and progress of the most fortunate empires since the beginning of time. We have imagined, in our unprecedented prosperity, that we should never be moved, that we should never be in adversity, and that the divine judgments would fail to overtake us for our national sins. We have been justly punished for that vain-glorious boasting, which has long excited the ridicule of the trans-Atlantic nations.—Our Union, our wealth, our population, our rapid territorial extension, have puffed us up with a pride and conceit, and filled us with a false security, so foolish and heaven-daring, that it has at last provoked the judgments of God. Not that it is the purpose of the Most High to destroy this great Republic in its infancy, and with all the great providential ends of its existence unaccomplished. We cannot believe this; the founding of the English Colonies in North America, their subsequent independence and union cost too great a price, and were marked in their progress with too many tokens of the ulterior purposes of the divine providence to allow so disastrous a conclusion. Are not the prayers of the early Colonists, from the Bay of Massachusetts to the Gulf of Mexico—of the Puritans of the North, the Presbyterians of the middle Colonies, and the Huguenots of the South—yet had in remembrance before God? Are not their tears "preserved in His bottle?" Are not the graves of the founders of the Republic, of the men who gathered the feeble, distracted and insolvent States of this continent into one great empire too fresh, as yet, for the destruction of the mighty work, accomplished by their wisdom, foresight and mutual forbearance? Are the counsels of the Father of his country so soon forgotten? Have the people of the United States been so suddenly bereft of their characteristic sagacity in all that concerns their material interests, as to plunge with their eyes open into the bottomless abyss of secession and dis-union? Will they submit for any length of time to any movement in that direction? Not until all patriotism is extinguished, not until all perception of national and individual interests is utterly lost, not until they are prepared to dishonor the graves of the dead who fell in every battlefield from Bunker Hill to Yorktown, and from Yorktown to the swamps of South Carolina, "where rang the shouts of Marion's men;" nay, more, not until they pour contempt upon the memory of the men who fell in the last war upon the Niagara frontier, and in the battle of New Orleans, can this Union be finally and hopelessly destroyed. Why, the bones of the hero of New Orleans would rattle in their coffin at such a consummation. Tennesee must remove the remains of Andrew Jackson from her soil, if she secedes, for his grave is a perpetual protest against disunion. How swiftly fled the unholy spectre of treason before the eagle eye and iron will of the stern old Patriot, when, in the proper exercise of his authority as Chief Magistrate, he exorcised it by the strong hand.

It is with this view of the subject, because we believe that God is chastising us in mercy as well as in wrath, for ever the Divine Providence presents to us a mingled cup of judgments and mercies, —because no great people or nation have ever reached the end of their progress or the maturity of their power, without passing through the fires of affliction, and undergoing the throes of intestine convulsions quite as formidable as the worst that threaten us —that we have adopted the language of the Supreme Governor addressed to his ancient people, the Hebrews, while smarting under the rod of Divine chastisement. The trials which threaten us are not to be met by dismay, despondency and terror,—these can only exasperate the malady of the body politic,—these can only lead to pusillanimous counsels and undecided action,—rather let us hear this voice from Him who led our Fathers to this continent and planted here a great nation, developing for the benefit of mankind a perfection of civil and religious liberty, before held unattainable. "When thou passest through the waters, I will be with thee, and through the rivers they shall not overflow thee. When thou walkest through the fire thou shalt not be burned, neither shall the flame kindle upon thee. Fear not, for I am with thee. I will bring thy seed from the East and gather thee from the West. I will say to the North give up, and the South keep not back."

While we humble ourselves before God by humiliation, fasting and prayer, let us lay aside our despondency, let us take refuge under the shadow of the wing of the Almighty, exclaiming, "God is our refuge and our strength, a very present help in every time of trouble, therefore will we not fear, if the earth were removed, though the mountains were carried into the depths of the sea." In the infancy of that great Republic of antiquity, which traversed three continents with its victorious arms, which conquered all that was worth conquest in Europe, Asia and Africa, intestine commotions repeatedly threatened its existence. What reader of history has forgotten the numerous exigencies in which the Roman people were compelled, by threatened disruption, to invest a Dictator with absolute power for a time, with the injunction, "to see that the Republic took no detriment." Who has forgotten the civil wars between the Patricans and the Plebians, deluging the streets of the "Eternal City" with blood? Nor did these difficulties entirely disappear until the wonderful vitality of the Republic and the love of liberty disappeared under the despotisms of the Cæsars. The very vigor of the body politic will produce eruptions in youthful and expanding Empires. There may be an excessive vitality, producing dangerous symptoms, and shall we cower before the first irregular action of these exuberant forces? Why, it was a standing maxim of the statesmen and people of Rome, "never to despair of the Republic," no matter if the enemy was at their gates—no matter if civil war was desolating their hearths. Shall the great Christian Republic of the 19th century, of which Rome was the archetype, manifest less courage and less resolution in the presence of similar dangers? Is modern history less instructive? How often has that great nation, which has girdled the earth with her colonies, from whom we boast our own descent, been rent by intestine commotions and desolated by civil wars, the last of which that placed William and Mary upon the throne of Great Britain, was within the memory of men living in our revolutionary era. What perpetual desolations for the last eighty years have made France a field of blood and a place of skulls, and yet she is to-day at the head of the continental powers of Europe, prosperous and progressive. Shall we fold our hands in fear and despair, because that which has occurred in all vigorous nationalities, has happened to us,—because the judgments with which God has chastened all nations for "pride, fulness of bread and abundance of idleness," have fallen deservedly on us "for reproof, for correction and instruction in righteousness?" No! no! Let us gird up the loins of our minds. God does not call us to the spirit of fear, but "of power and a sound mind." Let us have no more whining, no more irresolute counsels, no more desponding prophecies of ruin; in such a crisis, let us show ourselves men, worthy sons of the sires who faced the terrors, both of a foreign and civil war, in their desperate struggle for freedom and union. For what was the contest between the Whigs and Tories of the revolutionary era, but the worst form of a civil war, in which it was not section against section, North against South, East against West, but household against household; nay, worse, it was a war at the hearth, son against father and father against son. Are we so degenerate as to faint in the first day of adversity? Truly, in such a case, our "strength is small" and we may well become a prey to "treason's stratagems and spoils."

But it may be said, "this is a day of fasting, humiliation and prayer, in which we are called to look at the sad side of the present convulsions which threaten the integrity of our Union and the permanency of our government." Truly it is a day of humiliation, the setting apart of which was a highly proper act of the Executive, whatever else may have been neglected; but fasting and prayer do not imply irresolution and cowardice. The Puritans, in their deadly struggle with the Stuarts, fasted and prayed to some purpose; the soldiers of Cromwell, who carried Bibles in their knapsacks and made conventicles of their military quarters, were the bravest of the brave. It becomes us, indeed, to repent of our sins, to retrace our steps, where we have been wrong, to implore the divine guidance, and then to face our difficulties with the courage and constancy of a true Christian patriotism.

We shall endeavor, in the first place, to improve the present occasion by a brief consideration of some of the causes of the discords which have resulted in convulsions which threaten the perpetuity of our Union and our institutions, and endeavor, in the second, to point out the remedies.

Anterior to the revolution, the Colonies were existing under different forms of social life. The history of the introduction of African slavery is familiar. It was at first forced upon the colonists by the mother country and afterwards extended by the ship owners of New England, who found the importation of slaves from the west coast of Africa a highly profitable speculation. At the time when our present Constitution was framed and adopted, there was no substantial difference of opinion in the theoretical views of slavery between the North and the South. In some of the Northern States it was not abolished until long after the union; in all the States it was admitted to be an evil which would disappear by gradual emancipation in the process of time. No public sentiment in any part of the United States denounced the system as in itself sinful, and its abolition was simply a question of expediency with reference to its influence upon the white race and their material and moral interests. There was no dissension in respect to slavery at that time among the various denominations of Christians; North and South, the prevailing sentiment appears to have been that African servitude, existing under the form and by the sanction of law, was a valid institution under which both masters and slaves had their duties and their rights to be enforced by the Church of Christ, precisely as they are in the New Testament by Apostolic example and authority. No considerable body of Christians doubted that the action of the Savior and the Apostles in dealing with the relation of master and slave, as they dealt with other legal existing relations was binding upon the Church.

On the other hand, it was with equal unanimity maintained that slavery is not the *highest* form of Christian civilization or of social life; that while it is tolerated in both Testaments it is not expected to be permanent or perpetual; that while it is providentially and scripturally allowed, because it is *one of the means* by which inferior and indolent races have been and are elevated by enforced subjection to labor and law, yet its abandonment was to be expected whenever its ends were fully accomplished. Both North and South, it was agreed that slavery must at some time cease, and that a system of free labor was undoubtedly to be preferred whenever it could be safely and judiciously accomplished. It was felt and acknowledged on all hands, that there were inherent dangers and difficulties in the system of servitude, more particularly where there was a large preponderance of the slave population. That these moderate, just and Christian views of the subject were entertained by the founders of the Republic in both sections of the country, does not admit of a doubt. The debates in the Convention which formed our excellent Constitution, establish this beyond all controversy. This agreement in sentiment was one basis of the Union, and led to the mutual concessions by which free and slave States were brought together in indissoluble Union.

A primary cause of the present disorders is the abandonment by multitudes both North and South of these moderate views,—views in accordance with scripture, reason and experience.

More than thirty years since, a class of men in the North commenced a crusade against the South and Southern institutions, denouncing slavery as the "sum of all villianies" and the slaveholder as the greatest of all villians. The vocabulary of abuse was ransacked for epithets to heap upon our Southern brethren. Kidnappers, murderers and thieves were among the mildest terms applied to them by these pseudo philanthropists, whose hatred of the master was far more apparent than their love of the slave. Abandoning utterly the scriptural mode of dealing with slavery, refusing the teachings and example of the Apostles who had to do with in its worst forms, they outraged equally decency and common sense in their bitter denunciations and fanatical violence. These extreme men whose infidel tendencies, then predicted, have since become patent and apparent to all were never numerous in any section, but they made up in noise what they wanted in numbers. Christian denominations began at length to be influenced by this continued clamor, many sincere but injudicious and impulsive men in the ministry and membership of various churches were led to believe that these brawlers had really advanced to a ***higher standard of duty*** than had the Christian church; they were told this so often that they began to believe it. What was the Gospel of Rosseau and the French Encyclopedists and Jacobins, they strangely mistook for the Gospel of Christ, and this was the entering wedge of division in several denominations, resulting in the secession of the Northern from the Southern branch.

On the other hand, besides the natural exasperation felt by our brethren of the slave States in view of such treatment, there grew out of it as another result, a disposition on the part of extreme men at the South to glorify slavery. This was at first by way of retaliation, but afterwards, and by a natural process, it became the settled conviction of these men that slavery was 'Heavens' first law' of society, that there was in the future nothing higher or better—that their social condition was nearly millenial and that all communities, and the North especially, would do well to adopt the slave code, in which alone, they contended, is the perfection of human society. The extremists of one party made slavery the image of Hell, every master a demon and every slave a martyr to the lash. Drawing upon their imaginations for their facts, they filled the North with horrid tales and hideous pictures, and came at last by constant repetition to believe the fictions generated in their heated fancies. The extremists of the Southern side made the social condition of a slave State the image of Paradise, every master a pattern of gentleness, every slave a model of obedience. To these extreme opinions and their effect upon the people, both North and South, may be traced unquestionably the origin of the present disturbed condition of our common country. The first direct blow struck at our Union was inflicted, I am sorry to say it—but truth compels me to bear this testimony—by those Northern churches who virtually excommunicated their Southern brethren, saying in the arrogant spirit of the Pharisee, 'Stand aside, for I am holier then thou,' and this too with the *inheritance of the profits* of the slave trade in their possession and the proceeds of the sale of what they are pleased to call the 'human chattel' in their pockets ; for in the abolition of slavery in the Northern Colonies and States, sufficient time was always given the master to dispose of his slaves at the South, which was done in most cases by the virtuous Northerners whose descendants and heirs are now so abhorrent of property in man!

But, besides the unnecessary and unchristian antagonism upon the moral and religious questions involved in the existence of slavery, there has been a constantly increasing political jealousy between the two sections, which has materially aided in producing the present disastrous state of things. Instead of rejoicing over the unprecedented prosperity which God has given our common country, many at the North have had a feverish jealousy of the ascendancy of Southern statesmen in the national counsels. They have not alleged that the country was badly governed, but that the population and progress of the Southern States in comparison with the greater increase of the North did not warrant their overshadowing influence. The fact has been overlooked that this was the necessary result of the superior sagacity of the South in sending their best men to Washington and keeping them there, while the election often of inferior representatives and the principle of rotation in office, prevailing among all political parties at the North, has resulted in the natural predominance of those who by their ability and long experience were best prepared to guide the ship of state.

Now it is my solemn conviction, that this political ascendancy of the South, solely the fruit of the folly of the North, has had more to do with the result of the recent presidential election than all the abolition theories and all the abolition speeches with which the Northern States have been afflicted for the last thirty years. There never has been,—I do not believe there ever will be,—a major ity of Northern voters, disposed to disturb the social economy of the South, or who would, knowingly, lend themselves to a violation of the rights of the slave states under the constitution. The unhappy jealousy of southern predominance has far more influence with northern men, than the outcry against slavery. The truth is, Abolitionism proper has had its day at the North and is in a feeble and declining condition, and is destined, if let alone, to die the natural death of all such fanaticisms.

On the other hand, our Southern bretheren have been jealous of the increasing predominance of the North in population, and of the rapid increase of free states, disturbing the balance which they fondly hoped to maintain, at least in the Senate. They have undertaken to contend with the laws of nature, and the course of the divine providence, by which the West and North West have been occupied, and are now filling up with a hardy population from the despotisms of the old World, who can not only live but grow rich where a planter and his servants would starve.* This unnatural and unreasonable sectional jealousy is one of the initiating causes which has aided in producing the calamities which have called us together to day, to implore the divine forgiveness, and the removal of the divine judgments.

A third cause which we name in this connection, is the attempted violation of the Constitution by several of the Northern States, in respect to the rendition of fugitive slaves. That the constitution guarantees to the South the return of fugitive slaves is not denied. This was one of the compromises, and one of the conditions on which the Union was established. The attempted secession at Charleston, which is in fact rebellion against the general

---

* The territorial question is an offshoot of these extreme views. Massachusetts sends her free soil men, with rifles, into Kansas to keep out the *horrible* institution of slavery, while South Carolina and other Slave States force an unnatural colonization, in a like antagonistic spirit, sending her slavery propagandists, with bowie knives and blacks, to establish the '*divine*' institution, where the conditions of climate and soil are utterly opposed to its success. Theoretically the question now is whether slavery, under the Constitution, follows the 'lex loci,' or whether it exists by virtue of the organic law without any special enactment to legalize it. Several feasible methods have been proposed for the settlement of this irritating controversy. The plan of Judge Douglas, to give to the inhabitants of every Territory the sole right to determine this question, has long been before the country; even the Chicago platform does not preclude this plan of adjustment. The recent proposition of that venerable statesman and true patriot, Senator Crittenden, of Kentucky, would, in my opinion, be entirely acceptable to the great majority of Northern men. The only department of the government, in which it would be possible to secure in perpetuity to the South an equality in representation, is the judiciary.

By an amendment of the organic law it might be made imperative upon the President and Senate to appoint an equal number of the Judges of the Supreme Court from the two sections, so that the free and slave states would be always equally represented in that august tribunal, which as the Court of last resort, has the final decision of all questions arising under the Constitution, and is really the only *Supreme* power in the State. It might be further provided that all questions arising under the Constitution in regard to slavery, and in respect to the constitutionality of State enactments, and the rendition of fugitive slaves, should be decided by a bench composed equally of Northern and Southern Judges and that all such questions should be *privileged*, and receive the *immediate* attention and *speedy* adjudication of the tribunal. The high character of the Supreme Court—the fact that the judges are placed beyond the heat of mere party strife, and have a reputation to sustain before the country and the world, which must be dearer to them than mere sectional sentiment or approbation, would undoubtedly enable them, with a good degree of unanimity, to decide these exciting questions without delay. Where can they be settled so fairly and so satisfactorily?

government, is the natural result of this constructive treason at the North, for it is in the nature of things, that one treason should beget another; that the abandonment of constitutional compacts in one State, should provoke open insurrection in another. Can Massachusetts and Vermont expect to retain the blessings of the Union, and enforce its authority upon others, while they set the example of state legislation against the supreme law? Those who are engaged in, and justify such legislation, dishonor the graves of their fathers, they violate the sacred compact of the dead, they rend a covenant made before Earth and Heaven, before angels and men, upon which rests the peace and prosperity of more than thirty millions of souls; they seek to blot out the last hope, and the last experiment of a republican government, strong enough to occupy a place among the great nations of the earth. Are not these violations of good faith provocative of the divine indignation? Shall not God judge and avenge himself of such a people as this?

The counter legislation and violence of the South, while it cannot be justified, for one wrong can never justify another, is yet a natural consequence of the attempt at the North to evade and nullify one of the compacts of the constitution. Nor can their natural sensitiveness in regard to servile insurrections, justify the outrageous and indiscriminate violence which has disgraced portions of the South, in their barbarous treatment of innocent Northern men, without the forms of law, or even the color of provocation. Such conduct serves as an apology for their traducers: it tends to alienate their friends, and call down upon them the just judgments of God. There is a tone of bravado, a glorying in monstrous acts of violence, a sneering at Northern thrift, an impeachment of Northern courage, on the part of a portion of the press at the South, which is creating and exasperating a sectional feeling at the North, drifting us on to a bloody collision. That this is not an indication of the general temper of the South, I know from a recent residence of many months in a cotton-growing State. There is not a more generous, hospitable, chivalrous people on the face of the earth. The ardent sun of the tropics has indeed communicated to them some of its heat, and they are quick and impulsive in their friendships and enmities; but they are ever ready to retract an erroneous opinion, or correct a false judgment. The church of God has nowhere more faithful and eloquent ministers, nowhere more exemplary and benevolent communicants. That the great body of the Southern people are not directly responsible for the gasconade of a class of politicians and editors, who offend both the taste and the moral feeling of the North, appears very plainly from the discourse of the Rev. Dr. Dabney, of the South, upon the occasion of a fast recently appointed by the Synod of Virginia. After describing scenes in the French Revolution, he says :

" Now I say unto you in all faithfulness, that the reckless and incapable men whom you have weakly trusted with power or influence, have already led us far on towards similar calamities. They have bandied violent words those cheap weapons of petulant feebleness; they have justified aggression; they have misrepresented our tempers and principles—answered, alas, by equal misrepresentations and violence in other quarters—until multitudes of honest men, who sincerely suppose themselves as patriotic as you think yourselves, are really persuaded that in resisting your claims, they are but rearing a necessary bulwark against lawless and arrogant aggressions. Four years ago, an instance of unjust and wicked insolence was avenged, on the floor of the Senate of the United States, by an act of violence most unrighteous and illjudged. And now, not so much that rash and sinful act of retaliation, but the insane, wicked, and insulting justification of it generally made by southern secular prints, directed by reckless boys, or professed duellists, a justification abhorred and condemned by almost all decent men in our section, is this day carrying myriads of votes, (of men who, if not thus outraged, might have remained calm and just towards us,) for the cause whose triumph you deprecate. Thus the miserable game goes on; until at last, blood breaks out, and the exhausted combatants are taught in the end, by mutually inflicted miseries, to pause and consider, that they are contending mainly for a misunderstanding of each other.

" Whereunto can all this mutual violence grow? Do not the increasing anger and prejudice, which seem so fast ripening on both sides for a fatal collision, tell you too plainly? And when these rash representatives of yours in our halls of legislation and our newspapers, shall have sown the wind, who shall reap the whirlwind? When they have scattered the dragon's teeth, who must meet the horrent crop they will produce? Not they alone; but you, your sons, your friends and their sons. So that these misleaders of the people, while you so weakly connive at their indiscretions, may be indirectly preparing the weapon which is to pierce the bosom of your fair-haired boy: and summoning the birds of prey, which are to pick out those eyes whose joy is now the light of your happy homes, as he lays stark on some lost battle-field. For God's sake then—for your own sakes, for your children's sake, arise—declare that from this day, no money, no vote, no influence of yours, shall go to the maintenance of any other counsels than those of moderation, righteousness and manly forbearance."

To these solemn and prophetic admonitions, the North no less than the South, would do well to take heed. It is to some extent with us as it is with them. A class of politicians and editors are ever fomenting, especially in New England, the discords of the times, sowing the dragon's teeth of jealousy, suspicion and hatred, provoking a storm which they have no power to quell and no true patriotism or courage to meet. The "boys and duellists" of the South have no monopoly of the "Satanic press": we have amongst us those who are aiding in the unholy work of scattering fire-brands, arrows and death; men wanting principle and bread; men who, like Nero, are capable of fiddling amid the flames which they have kindled—amid the falling towers of our Union and our Constitution. I am glad to except our local press from this incendiarism.

With this brief review of some of the causes which have led to the present convulsed condition of the country, we hasten to consider the remedies of the evils which seem to imperil our national existence.

In the text, the Supreme Ruler addresses words of encouragement to the Hebrews, at the very moment when the nation was smarting under his judgments. "Fear not, for I am with thee. I will bring thy seed from the East, and gather thee from the West; I will say to the North, give up, and to the South, keep not back." May we not apply these words to our own case by way of encouragement, and interpret them as a promise to gather together the true patriots of our land from the East and the West, to stand in the breach and stay the tides of faction and disunion? Is not the language of His providence to-day, to us, "I will say to the North, Give up, and to the South, Keep not back? Without greatly violating the original meaning of these words in their scriptural connection, may we not apply them, by way of accommodation, to our own case, and see in them the precise and only feasible solution of our difficulties?

It is literally true that God is saying in his providence to the North 'give up,' and to the South 'keep not back.' It is quite obvious that unless the North is prepared to *give up* her antagonism to the constitutional guarantees for the rendition of the fugitive slaves of the South, unless the free States give up their unlawful intermeddling with the domestic affairs and local institutions of their neighbors, a violent and bloody solution of our difficulties cannot be avoided. It is equally true that if the South *'keep back'* from accepting the proper guarantees for the future that their constitutional rights shall be maintained, there can be no peaceable settlement of our national animosities. There can be no doubt that there is an increasing disposition at the North to remove all just grounds of complaint, to repeal all unconstitutional State laws, and to frown upon all intermeddling with the social system of the South. We implore our Southern brethren not to 'keep back' from these proffers of peace and good will. We solemnly assure them that the element of abolitionism is by no means predominant in the party which is about to assume the administration of the government and that however alarming the election of a sectional candidate to the chief magistracy may be assumed to be, it nevertheless becomes them to wait and see what course is taken by the incoming administration. To move in advance of this is as unwise as it is dangerous. It would indicate a foregone conclusion, a secession *for other reasons than those avowed*, and justify the allegation that there is at the bottom of the secession movement only the animosity of baffled politicians and the ambition of reckless demagogues, who hope by an act of treason to found a new Empire in which they can monopolize all offices of trust and of honor. If the North will at once 'give up' where they are wrong, and the South 'keep not back' from a fair concession, if both will suffer "bygones to be bygones" then a peaceable settlement of our difficulties may be expected, a settlement worthy an enlightened christian people, acceptable to God, and over which there will be joy in Heaven. But while we earnestly desire and pray for this peaceful solution of our troubles, it becomes us to look beyond this and see what other remedies may be found, in case this proves impossible.

I am compelled to confess my amazement at much that has been said in high places and sacred places, from the Executive chair and in the Senate, from the forum and the pulpit, in regard to *peaceable secession*, peaceful division and the peaceful abandonment of our union and government which has been represented substantially, as incapable of resisting disintregration from treason. If this be so, we have no government, but merely the shadow or simulacrum of one, which ought to be scouted down and abandoned at once. Whatever a false and sickly sentimentalism may pretend, however it may ape the peace and good will of the gospel, nothing is more certain than that the scriptural and Christian doctrine of government is utterly at war with the imbecile and pusillanimous conduct inculcated by this new political dogma. The Apostle declares that " the powers that be are ordained of God," in which is intended all existing governments, whether administered under despotic or democratic forms, " Whosoever," continues the Apostle, " resisteth the power, resisteth the ordinance of God; and they that resist shall receive to themselves condemnation." Again, in the same connection, it is said of rulers, meaning thereby governments in their executive action, "for he beareth not the SWORD in vain, for he is the minister of God, a revenger to execute wrath upon him that doeth evil." "Wherefore," continues the Apostle, " ye must needs be subject not only for wrath but also for conscience sake." The idea of any reserved right of secession of a State is incompatible with the existence of a general government, at war with the terms of the Constitution itself and can hardly be maintained with sincerity by any reflecting man. The Union could never have been formed with this reservation, by the people of the United States—for our Union is not of the States but of the people—nor could it have been adopted, with a right of secession. Such a proviso would have been a nullification of the Constitution at its very inception, and made it but a rope of sand. If we have a government that is unable to protect itself against insurrection, let it be abandoned at once. If our Union cannot be maintained under Republican forms, let us have centralization, a monarchy and a standing army, for these evils cannot compare with the absolute ruin that must follow our division into numerous petty, distracted States, which, like the Republics of South America, will become the scorn of mankind.

The recent attempted secession of South Carolina would be a mere farce, notwithstanding the earnest and treasonable temper of its leaders, were not the example almost certain to be followed by the adjacent Gulf States. South Carolina contains less than an eightieth part of the white population of the United States. She is the Massachusetts of the South. It often happens that those who hate each other are much alike, and so it is with the Bay State of the North and the Palmetto State of the South. Both abound with glorious revolutionary recollections, both have dishonored them—both were foremost in accomplishing the great work of Union—both have done what they could to destroy it—both have produced an extraordinary number of able men, and both have alike suffered from their ultra and fanatical opinions, either in politics or morals ; both have been extreme advocates of State rights —both have attempted to nullify the Constitution of the United States—both are denunciatory, turbulent and violent, the one in word the other in deed—both are filled with self conceit, the one styling Boston the Athens of the North, the other claiming that Charleston is the Thermopylæ of the South! In both, the most extreme opinions in regard to society and government prevail ; the one maintaining that the perfection of civilization is found in a community with one white man, the master of a hundred negroes; the other insisting that the beau ideal of philanthropy is only seen where the rights and interests of a hundred whites are sacrificed for the benefit of a single African. To these States, in their mutual likeness and their mutual hatred, more than any other, we owe the origin of the impending collision!

God forbid we should be compelled to resort to the stern arbitrament of the sword. The appeal to arms is the last remedy against the destruction of the Republic—it is a sad one, but better than none. A civil, and even a servile war, with all their horrors, are infinitely preferable to anarchy; no sacrifices are too great for the preservation of our nationality, without which we are but dismembered and worthless fragments of a once glorious body whose dissevered limbs will be a perpetual stench in the world's atmosphere. It has been said, indeed, that the forcible suppression of secession, which is but another name for insurrection, must be followed by an alienation of feeling and create bitter animosities which would render a future and forced Union worthless. This is plausible at first view, but is contradicted by uniform and universal experience. Have the civil contests of England left behind them any such results? Are the Vendean Provinces of France less faithful and less attached to their nationality to-day, because, within the memory of multitudes now living, they were desolated by fire and sword in a protracted civil war, the atrocities of which are almost unparalleled in the history of intestine convulsions? Are not geographical boundaries and commercial necessities, a common language and a common faith, more invincible than human passions, and stronger than the madness of any hour or any age? Does any sane man really believe that the permanent separation of this great country is possible with an Anglo-Saxon race for its occupants, and with all the material interests of commerce, and all the elements of power dependent upon its union? Never were two sections of a great country more mutually dependent on each other than the slave and free States. The cotton of the South has almost uniformly paid the enormous balances which our foreign trade has annually left against us through our excessive importations, while the products of the North have always found their nearest and best markets in the slave States,—they are in fact a necessity, and must be while cotton and tobacco continue to be their great staples. The rebellion of States against the General Government is like the revolt of the members against the head, and can never, in the nature of the case, be permanent or finally successful.

But it may be replied, who can foretell the issue of such a struggle—who can say to whom, in such a war, the Most High will award the victory? Doubtless, the issue of all events is, in a degree, hidden in the womb of time, and in the purpose of God; but there are some things so plain that he "that runneth may read," in which "the way-faring man, though a fool, need not err."

I would I had a voice to penetrate the South, to warn them of impending danger. They would recognize it as the voice of a friend who has ever defended their rights and vindicated their character; of one who, ten years ago, delivered a discourse in this place, which had an almost unprecedented circulation throughout the country, in which the scriptural view of slavery was presented, and the rights of the South to a restoration of their fugitive slaves maintained. From the then Chief Magistrate of the Nation,—our eminent fellow citizen, Millard Fillmore,—whose wise and impartial administration of the government is acknowledged by all, I received a letter of thanks, in which he recognized this discourse, however humble the origin, as one of the instrumentalities of peace in that stormy time. As a tried and known friend, I would warn my Southern brethern of the perils of their position in their attempts to revolutionize the government. I would ask them in the first place to consider in what position the Gulf States would be placed by the act of secession. The mildest measure possible with any administration, not itself in league to destroy the Union, would be to close the ports of entry in every seceeding State. This blockade, easily accomplished by a few war steamers, could not be resisted by the Gulf States; they have neither ships nor ship-builders, and before they could obtain either, they must become insolvent and powerless, as the result of their isolation. Let them look this thing fairly in the face; for it is certain to follow, as it is certain that the government will not commit suicide. Let them look at it in another point of view. The opening of the Gulf ports as free ports of entry would at once destroy the revenue of the country, and paralyze the commerce of the nation—virtually closing every port of every non-seceeding State. Do the South imagine that this will be permitted for an hour? Let our Southern friends take another view of the case. They propose secession as a defence of the slave economy; is not this a capital mistake? A far-seeing statesman of Tennesee has declared that SECESSION IS ABOLITION! Without here entering upon the argument, it will be sufficient to suggest to the South whether they are not doing effectually the very thing which the abolitionists have vainly attempted for the last thirty years? Will a brave man commit suicide because his life is threatened by a ruffian hitherto baffled of his purpose? "I speak to wise men, judge ye what I say!" Will the border States fall, with their eyes open, into the snare of secession, giving the Gulf States all the profit of the revolt, if there be any, and assuming to themselves the immediate and certain ruin which must follow? Will they undertake to fortify and guard a frontier of a thousand miles against the daily and nightly flight of negroes deluded by a fancied elysium at the North?

Let us say in this connection, that the true friends of the South, outside of their own territory, are all at the North. There is no nation or community on earth to whom they can look for sympathy or from whom they can expect aid, in this proposed exodus from the Union. The fanaticism and prejudices of the European nationalities are far more inveterate than the antagonism of the Northern States. Attempted secession will unite all parties, and all persons in the free states against them, not on account of slavery, but because they will be constrained to treat the enemies of the Government and the Constitution as their enemies; not because they love the South less, but the Union more. With the exception of a few rabid abolitionists who hate all government and all law, there will be an entire unanimity in the free States in resistance to the proposed disruption of the Country. Can the slave States afford to remain outside the community of nations, to be treated as pirates at sea by the naval powers of the world, if they should succeed in opening the slave trade by a successful attempt to establish a Southern confederacy? For that this will be the first demand of the Gulf states, and their first action upon succesful secession, no man can doubt who is familiar with public sentiment in the extreme South. Are the Border states prepared to accept this action and incur this odium, and sacrifice their local interests to a foreign slave trade? Unless they are prepared to do this, there will be a fresh secession and a new division among the slave States themselves within twelve months after the inauguration of the proposed Southern Republic.

Truth compels me to say another thing, which I would gladly omit, did not the present crisis demand on the part of the South a most careful consideration of it at the present moment. I mean the inherent and unavoidable weakness of slave States in a civil contest with free States. Now, I have lived among my Southern brethern; I know their courage, always bordering upon rashness. I know their virtues. I know that the slave, both socially and morally, is in a far better condition at the South than the free black at the North; for the former is treated *as a human being*, with familiarity and kindness, and instructed in the gospel which proffers alike to master and servant the blessings of salvation; the other, not so much by any fault of his own, is made an outcast and a vagabond, the very Pariah of our Northern civilization. These things I know and confess, but I know also, and reflecting men every where know, that an ignorant people in servitude, however kindly treated, do not well understand their own interests; that an imaginative race like the African are easily excited and deluded by ideas of liberty and an Ethiopian Paradise at the North, which, though it fades away like a mirage at their approach, still dazzles their vision at a distance. Cannot the South see that a civil war, to which all things seem now tending, must *inevitably* render the servile population restless and uneasy, and at last dangerous? I have not the least idea that a Northern army would incite or favor insurrection, but they could have no power to prevent it, and in the Gulf States at least, the white population are not sufficiently numerous to engage in a civil war under a state of things which would require every citizen to enrol himself among the police, organized to watch over the slave.

A civil war must necessarily disturb the very foundations of society in the Slave States, while the Free States could easily spare more than half a million of men, "the cankers of a calm world and a long peace"—whose absence would not weaken us or disturb the movement of a single factory, or take a mechanic from a solitary workshop. Certainly, it becomes any people, however courageous and resolute, however justly offended, to count the cost, before they make the plunge into the gulf of a civil—to which must be added, the horrors of a servile war. Nor is this commendable forethought without the Divine warrant. Luke 14, 31, "What King going to war against another King sitteth not down first and consulteth whether he be able with ten thousand to meet him who cometh against him with twenty thousand. Or else, while the other is yet a great way off, he sendeth an Ambassage and desireth conditions of peace."

Nor will it be unwise for the North to consider what particular sectional profit there will be, even in their success. They may save the Union, but at a loss which it will take a generation to repair. Suffer me to repeat, at this time, what I said ten years since in this place, in the discourse before referred to, as applicable now as it was then. "There are no visionaries so wild as those who dream that this vast Empire can be disunited peacefully, or that peace can ever be maintained between the North and the South, under separate governments, with all the old memories, the bitter prejudices, the unavoidable rivalries, the unceasing disputes of jurisdiction, with the mouth of the Mississippi in one territory and its sources in the other, and with the o inous slave question, embittered a thousand fold by the dismemberment of the country. If, in this unnatural contest, the North should prevail over the South, it would be by making a desert of the territory from the Potomac to the Gulf of Mexico, and by the destruction of both the races who now occupy it, a victory—as a sectional triumph barren of glory—the jest of tyrants, and the scorn of the world.

"I would appeal to the North and the South, by their common ancestry, by the august memories of the revolutionary struggle, by the bones of their fathers which lie mingled together at Yorktown and Saratoga, at Trenton and Charleston, by the farewell counsels of the immortal Washington, to lay aside their animosities and to remember that they are brethren. I would remind them that the Union has given us the blessings which we enjoy—that under its Flag our victories have been won; our borders extended; our wealth and population increased; our ships respected in every port of every sea, until our national progress has excited the admiration, or aroused the envy, of all the Nations and Potentates of the earth. I would warn them of that abyss of ruin which fanaticism and treason are opening beneath them; into which they would plunge our present fortunes and our future hopes. I would beseech them to stand by the Union, to obey the laws, to frown upon agitation, in this crisis of our beloved country. I would admonish them that failing to do this, failing to sustain the free institutions, and to regard the mutual compacts which we received from our fathers, we may expect as a consequence the curses of posterity, the contempt of the world, and the judgments of God."

But I must draw to a close. I have endeavored to speak plainly, sincerely and truly, without fear or favor of North or South, as a patriot and a christian, as a lover of my country, and as a servant of God. May the Almighty avert from us the horrors of a civil war, and if he calls us to pass through an affliction, from which no great nation has yet been exempted, may he give us grace to meet the crisis with courage and constancy, not in mortal terror, and with our heads bowed down as a bulrush. May God deliver our rulers from the 'spirit of fear,' and give them wisdom and courage according to their day and the crisis they are compelled to meet. May the clouds which have risen at the South, and which begin also to appear in our Northern horizon, discharge their electric fires before they meet in mid-heaven in a conflict which must darken the hopes of freedom throughout the world, a conflict which will bring mourning and woe into innumerable households, and fill the land with widows and orphans. Hear, O Lord, the prayer of thy people in the day of their calamity! accept their humiliation, avert from them thy threatened judgments, preserve the Union of these States, destroy not the people thou didst plant in the wilderness, whose dominions thou hast extended from ocean to ocean. Say unto us in the midst of the perils which surround us as thou didst to thy chosen people in the ancient days, "Fear thou not, for I am with thee, be not discouraged, for I am thy God; I will strengthen thee: yea, I will help thee; when thou passest through the waters I will be with thee; when thou walkest through the fire thou shalt not be burned, neither shall the flame kindle upon thee. Fear not, for I am with thee; I will bring thy seed from the East, and gather thee from the West. I will say to the North, give up, and to the South, keep not back." Amen and amen.

www.ingramcontent.com/pod-product-compliance
Lightning Source LLC
LaVergne TN
LVHW011627120826
845150LV00012B/2352
* 9 7 8 1 4 1 8 1 9 3 5 9 1 *